THEY SANG

AN ADVENT COURSE BASED ON THE FOUR SONGS IN THE CHRISTMAS STORY

AMY SCOTT ROBINSON

KEVIN MAYHEW LTD

INTRODUCTION

Have you ever wished the world was more like a musical, with characters bursting into song at the slightest provocation? In the nativity story, there are four sudden, Spirit-filled songs from the heart, and they're all still used in the rhythm of liturgy: Zechariah's song (the Benedictus) Mary's song (Magnificat) the song of the angels (Gloria in Excelsis) and Simeon's song (Nunc Dimittis).

These sudden songs, all filled with prophecy and praise, are wonderful to read during Advent because they contain all the expectations of what the Messiah would be like and his purpose in coming to earth. Because of that, they help us to look back to the first Christmas with wonder, through the eyes of the people who experienced it; and forward to a time when God will finally fulfil all of those expectations in the kingdom of heaven.

As you read and study together, I encourage you to join the song, recognising that God has given each of us the capacity for creativity and praise, and that the shouts of his children never go unheard.

NOTES FOR LEADERS

There is plenty of flexibility in these sessions to adapt them to your group, and how you use them may depend on numbers and on the confidence of the group. The Join The Song sections, in particular, may work best for you if you prepare them as a group reading by printing out parts and deciding on readers in advance; or you may be able to have a go at them in the session without preparing; or you may prefer to read them yourself, or to drop them altogether and use the canticle suggested instead.

Some of the Response sections may take a little more preparation than a conventional small group study, both to ensure that you have the resources needed, and to be confident that you understand the creative task and can explain it to the group. Again, there is plenty of room for adaptation, and rather than give a strict form of words I have left it to you to decide the best way to present the task for your group.

The final workshop session is focused on Christmas more than Advent; if you have run the four sessions in the four weeks of Advent, you may end up coming back to the workshop during the Christmas season. The idea is to bring together elements of everything learned from the four songs to create a Christmas song of praise, either individually or as a group. But don't worry about ending up with a polished product. The main aim of the workshop is to revisit and consolidate the concepts from the Advent sessions, and there should be an air of celebration and play, rather than hard work!

SESSION ONE:
BENEDICTUS, A SONG OF SALVATION

BEGIN
Introduction

Luke's Gospel begins, not with the birth of Jesus, but with the curious story of Zechariah and Elizabeth, and the events leading up to the birth of their son, John. This child, Jesus' cousin, will become John the Baptist; and beginning the narrative with his birth marks out Luke's Gospel as one which contains a uniquely close, familiar view of Jesus, leading some scholars to speculate that Luke heard eyewitness accounts from Mary and other members of Jesus' immediate family.

In Luke's Gospel it is Zechariah, not Mary, who is the first to see an angel, hear the announcement of a birth and receive the name to be given to the unborn child. His reaction is to protest and ask for a sign: "How shall I know this? For I am an old man, and my wife is advanced in years." (Luke 1:18, NRSV) The sign the angel gives him is to take away his power of speech until the fulfilment of what has been said.

The order of events in the Gospel is that Mary then visits

Elizabeth, the unborn John leaping for joy in the presence of the unborn Jesus, and she sings the Magnificat; but we will come to that story in the next session and stick with Zechariah for now, because his song, as we will see, acts as a sort of pivot between the Old Testament and the New.

It's only when muted Zechariah scrawls the name 'John' on a writing tablet that his tongue is loosened again, and the sound that comes out is a song of praise and prophecy over his new son, a song that has been building up and growing in silence along with the unborn child. Zechariah remembers God's past promises and looks forward to their fulfilment in a song that crosses from old to new, from light to day, centring on John as if he stands at the dividing line between the two. He sings of redemption, salvation, holiness, righteousness and tender mercy.

OPENING QUESTION

What have been the biggest transitions in your life? Perhaps a move from education to employment, from single to married, from one place to another? Take a moment to say aloud or to write down some of the memories of what marked those transitions – the feelings, reasons, ceremonies and relationships. What changed and what stayed the same? Were your hopes or fears realised?

If you could go back in time to just before that transition, what would you tell your past self about what was to come?

WORSHIP

Pray

Zechariah was filled with the Holy Spirit and prophesied. Father, fill us with your Spirit now as we read and consider his song. You hold together the past and the future, our times are in your hands: be with each of us, Lord, and meet us wherever we find ourselves. Amen.

Sing

Here are some suggestions for hymns and songs which you could sing or listen to as you worship together:

- Lord, For The Years (Timothy Dudley-Smith)
- On Jordan's Bank the Baptist's Cry (Charles Coffin)
- Thy Hand, O God, Has Guided (E.H. Plumptre)
- Freedom Is Coming (trad. Spiritual)
- When I Was Lost (Kate and Miles Simmonds, Kingsway music)

Read

Luke 1:67-79

(And/or you may like to use this, or the following section to say, sing or chant a version of the Benedictus from the Book of Common Prayer or Common Worship: you will find it in the service of Morning Prayer.)

JOIN THE SONG

Blessed be the Lord
who looks on us with favour
remembering his word,
he raised a mighty saviour,
raised a mighty saviour

Chorus:
That we, being rescued from our foes
might serve him without fear
the mercy he promised in his holy covenant is here
and we will go out before the Most High to prepare his ways
in holiness and righteousness before him all our days

As for you, my child,
prepare each longing nation
for freedom from their sins
and knowledge of salvation,
knowledge of salvation

Chorus

Through God's tenderness,
in heaven a light is dawning
to guide our feet in peace
and turn dark night to morning,
turn dark night to morning

Chorus

TRACK AVAILABLE FOR DOWNLOAD AT
KEVINMAYHEW.COM/PRODUCTS/THEY-SANG

A D
1. Bles - sed be the Lord who
2. As for you, my child, pre -
3. Through his ten - der - ness in
3 E A
looks on us with fa - vour. Re -
pare each long - ing na - tion for
heav'n a light is dawn - ing to
5 A D
mem - ber - ing his word he
free - dom from their sins and
guide our feet in peace, and
7 E A
raised a migh - ty Sa - viour,
know - ledge of sal - va - tion,
turn dark night to morn - ing,
9 E D A7
raised a migh - ty Sa - viour.
know-ledge of sal - va - tion.
turn dark night to morn - ing.

12 A Chorus D A
That we, be - ing res - cued from our
14 D A D
foes, might serve him with - out
16 E A
fear. The mer - cy he pro-mised
18 D
in his ho - ly co - ve - nant__ is
20 E A
here. And we will go out be -
22 D A
-fore the Most__ High to pre-pare his

24 D A
ways in ho - li - ness___ and
26 D E7
right - eous - ness be - fore him all___ our
To verses 2 & 3
Last time
28 A A
days. days, in
31 A D
ho - li - ness___ and right - eous - ness be -
33 E7 A
-fore him all___ our days.

If it's not possible to sing this together, choose a different member of the group to read each verse out loud. Say the choruses together.

(Alternatively, you may like to use this space to say, sing or chant a version of the Benedictus from the Book of Common Prayer or Common Worship: you will find it in the service of Morning Prayer.)

EXPLORE

Read

The scramble for interval drinks is over, the bar is closing, the queue for the toilets has dwindled and the audience makes its way back into the auditorium. As people take their seats and the lights go down, the orchestra is already playing the entr'acte. It's a short piece of music, just long enough for the latecomers to shuffle back in past everyone's knees and get settled before the curtain goes up, and it contains snatches of all the songs you've heard in the musical so far – but it builds to the new tune of the second act opening song.

If the Old Testament were act one and the New Testament act two, Zechariah's song is the entr'acte. In almost every line, it contains echos from the prophets - Samuel, Isaiah, Jeremiah, Malachi and Micah all feature – and references to the story of Abraham, while hinting forward at all of these coming together in a person named the Most High, the Lord.

(If you'd actually like to look up all the references, I have listed them below. In a group, you could take one or two each. Before you do, though, have you noticed any echoes already? You can probably find some that aren't listed.)

The theme of the song is salvation. Zechariah remembers God's repeated promises to redeem, save and deliver his people, and says that they are being fulfilled. He echoes David's song of deliverance from his enemies (2 Samuel 22:3) and God's promise to Abraham that future generations of his family would be rescued from their oppressors (Genesis 15:13-14). But these stories of rescue from enemy nations are only foreshadowings of a much greater rescue, one from darkness and the shadow of death.

As Christians, we might think of salvation as a one-time event: a cataclysmic moment in history when we think of the cross, or a single moment in the lifetime of a person when we think in terms of coming to faith. But in Zechariah's song, salvation is something that has happened, is happening and will happen. It's a process and a story, both in the lives of individuals and for the world as a whole.

Zechariah's song resonates with the pronouncements that Jesus will make about the now-and-not-yet of God's kingdom. The song praises God for all the times his promises have been kept, and his people rescued, in the past – but still looks ahead with hope to the full completion of God's plan for humanity.

References to the Old Testament in Zechariah's song:

Zechariah	Old Testament
Luke 1:69 horn of salvation	2 Samuel 22:3
Luke 1:69 house of David	Isaiah 11:1, Jeremiah 23:5
Luke 1:71 saved from our enemies	Psalm 106:10
Luke 1:72 mercy promised to our fathers	Micah 7:20
Luke 1:73-74 promises to Abraham	Genesis 15:13-14; 22:16-18
Luke 1:75 holiness and righteousness	Genesis 18:19
Luke 1:76 go before the Lord to prepare his ways	Isaiah 40:3; Malachi 3:1
Luke 1:78 sunrise from on high	Malachi 4:2
Luke 1:79 light for those in darkness	Isaiah 9:2
Luke 1:79 a way of peace	Isaiah 9:7

Discuss

- Looking back over your life, what events or people could you thank God for?
- When do you think you have been in the most danger? What happened?
- Have you ever had the sense of being rescued from something, or having had a narrow escape?
- What are your greatest hopes at the moment – for the near and the distant future?
- What are the images, memories or associations that come to mind when you hear the word 'salvation'?

Respond

You can do this exercise privately if you're using this book by yourself. In a group, members might like to use their own journals, paper or the space provided here to draw their response while a leader reads the following poem and instructions out loud, giving time in between for the group to follow them. You could light a candle, play quiet music in the background and encourage members that this is time for them to spend with God: they won't need to share their responses with anyone else.

Steadfast

Her faith is a cathedral
built slowly, over generations,
stone by hand-placed stone.
The foundations are original,
but there was prayer already in this place
before them, and has been ever since.
The weaker parts have crumbled
and fallen away, or been lovingly repaired
and there have been many additions:
this once-austere cloister has a place for coffee now,
and modern windows look out over graves
where, from dead and long dead
flowers grow joyful with memories.
Now, although some saints have been defaced,
and despite the stained glass that never went
back in quite right after the war,
the cathedral towers over the city.
It's the first thing you notice, coming in.
Her visitors marvel at how strong a structure
was built so long ago
and without the help of all we know
these days.

In the poem, the cathedral is a metaphor for a person's life in faith. You are going to draw your life's cathedral. You don't need to label it, unless you want to: you know what each part means. It doesn't need to be a work of art. It is a prayer picture, for your eyes only.

First, consider the foundations as you draw the bottom few stones. Is there a moment in your life when faith began for you? What were your first influences? Have you always had a sense of spirituality or wonder, or is that something that has grown up later, or not at all for you?

As you sketch the shape of the cathedral, think about what shape faith takes for you now. Is it structured and supported by a community, or is it something you mainly keep private? Does it show up for festivals and special times, or in life's events? What has most shaped your life and the person you are?

Sketch in a cathedral door. Will you draw it open or closed – do you want to invite other people into your experience of God, or is it something deeply personal, just for you?

The stained glass windows in a cathedral often tell stories, not just from the Bible and saints' stories, but about the community and people who placed them there. Some of them are memorials. As you add them to your picture, consider: who are your saints, the people who have led, nurtured and influenced you the most? What memories stand out as part of your unique story? Are there people in those memories who are not with you any more?

When you have finished your sketch, imagine going into your cathedral. Perhaps you would light a candle, explore, or sit quietly for a while. In your imagination, you can share that experience with God. Thank him for the parts of your cathedral that you admire, the beauty in your life. Talk to him about the parts that have changed, or not come out as you would have planned. Remember with him the people and experiences that have built you, and look forward with him to all that is to come.

UNTIL NEXT TIME

Pray

Father, you have rescued us: help us to serve you without fear. You have saved us: help us to go out before you, preparing the way for you in the hearts and minds of your people. You are the dawn that enters the darkness of night: guide our feet in peace until morning. Amen.

Ponder

Can you sum up in one sentence what the birth of Jesus means for the world?

How about five words?

Three?

Bring your shortest attempt to share with the group next week.

Prepare

For next week, look ahead to the session's introduction and read either the Bible passage (Luke 1:39-56) or the Magnificat from the Book of Common Prayer (you will find it in evening prayer).

If you are going to follow the Response activity with a group next week, you may wish to ask the group to look out for articles of news which particularly touch or concern them over the week, and print or cut out newspaper clips to bring with them.

SESSION TWO:
MAGNIFICAT, A SONG OF JUSTICE

BEGIN
Introduction

The story of Mary's visit to Elizabeth is woven in with that of Zechariah and the angel: it happens after the births of both John and Jesus have been fortold, when Mary is in the very early days after her meeting with the angel Gabriel; and her cousin, although she is 'in her old age', is more than half way through her own miraculous pregnancy.

We are used to hearing, in Christmas services, a reading which begins "In the sixth month the angel Gabriel was sent from God to a city of Galilee named Nazareth, to a virgin..." (Luke 1:26-27 NRSV) Have you ever stopped to wonder, the sixth month of what? Luke is referring to Elizabeth's pregnancy, because he is still telling the story with which he began – of the birth of John the Baptist – and not yet that of Jesus. The whole framework of this part of the Gospel is Elizabeth's story rather than Mary's. That's why we have the beautiful moment, from Elizabeth's point of view, when the baby leaps inside her and she is filled with the Holy Spirit and knows that her unborn son has already recognised the son of God, just as the angel predicted to Zechariah (verses 15-16). And it's Elizabeth's exclamation – using the word 'blessed' three times as she greets Mary – that gives rise to the reply which is the Magnificat, Mary's song.

Mary has held it together up until now. We've seen her tentative, obedient response to Gabriel, and been told that she was 'greatly troubled' at the greeting from the angel. I wonder how carefully and secretly she kept all this to herself as she travelled to Elizabeth's house. Perhaps there was a little part of her that needed to see with her own eyes that Gabriel's news about her cousin was true – if it really was, then surely his news for her must be true, too. Or perhaps Mary sought comfort from the only other person on earth who could possibly begin to understand what had happened to her. Either way, Elizabeth's acceptance and affirmation unlock a deeper response from Mary, and her words pour out of her with joy, faith and a sense of relief.

OPENING QUESTION/ACTIVITY

What do you think is the biggest issue of social justice facing society today?

Share your responses and preparation from last week.

WORSHIP

Pray

Lord Jesus, you were tiny, but incarnate in Mary's womb when she sang this song of praise: you were with her in body and in spirit. Be with us, be among us now as we learn about your heart for justice, your kingdom and your plan for how the world should work. Help us to take up the challenge of living as citizens of that kingdom. Amen.

Sing

Here are some suggestions for hymns and songs which you could sing or listen to as you worship together:

- Tell Out My Soul (Timothy Dudley-Smith)
- The Angel Gabriel From Heaven Came (S. Baring-Gould)
- Jesus Christ Is Waiting (John Bell and Graham Maule)
- Blessed Be Your Name (Matt Redman)

Read

Luke 1:39-56. If you want to include the Annunciation, then start at verse 26.

(Alternatively, you may like to use this or the following space to say, sing, chant or listen to a version of the Magnificat from the Book of Common Prayer or Common Worship: you will find it in the service of Evening Prayer.)

JOIN THE SONG

This is a poem that could be read by one or many voices. It's inspired both by the Magnificat, and the Beatitudes from the Sermon on the Mount: the words of Mary and of her son, and how they chime together to describe a Kingdom in which the normal way of things is overturned.

I have suggested a way to read it with three voices: a questioner (Q) and two answering voices (A1 and A2) to stand for Mary and Jesus. You could add a third answering voice instead of going back to A1 in the final stanza; or use it as you wish.

The Kingdom's Down Here

Q: I can't think how to pray when I'm watching the news.
All humanity's hurting, divided and bruised.
And all I can say is: this world's a disaster.
A familiar prayer: 'Let God's kingdom come faster!'

A1: But the kingdom's down here, if you have eyes to see:
Like when God picks an unmarried teen refugee
To be pregnant, alone, with no family supporting,
She gets dumped by her man, and instead of aborting,
She sings! She rejoices! She calls herself blessed,
Says God scatters the proud, raises up the oppressed,
Knocks the powerful down, fills the hungry with food,
Sends the rich home with nothing. She says God is good
And remembers his mercy. And all of her hoping
Is how she is living, not just how she's coping.
She's seeing the world in this radical light;

In the Light of the World. It's because, not despite
The way that things are, that the kingdom shines through.
In the light of the world we can glimpse what is true.

Q: So where is the kingdom? When the mighty are strong,
When the hungry are starved, have we cause for a song?

A2: Yes! The song of the kingdom's the song of the blessed.
It goes: blessed are the losers. Blessed the distressed.
Blessed are the poor, the downtrodden, the slow,
The refugees running with nowhere to go,
They're all blessed. The grieving are blessed, and the weak,
The bullied, the broken, the unspoken meek,
Blessed are the victims. Blessed the oppressed,
Blessed are the stressed, blessed the depressed.
And blessed are the peacemakers. Blessed beyond measure
The pure-hearted ones who discover this treasure,
This parallel kingdom, invisible, true,
And bring it to blessing. And they could be you.

A1: For the kingdom's down here, if you have eyes to see,
With the hungry and poor, and in you, and in me.
For the kingdom is doing its mustard seed thing
Where a gaggle of losers who loved a dead king
Start to meet; washing feet; sacrificing their lives
Every day, like their king, always dying to rise.
Because here in this kingdom, it's all upside down.
The humblest are highest, the poor get the crown
And the winners who sprinted to be in first place
Are arriving to find that they lost the whole race

To the stragglers and limpers who loped at the back
And the ones who served drinks at the side of the track.
So don't worry. The kingdom is here. It's not gone.
It's existing in us. Love has already won.

(Alternatively, you may like to use this space to say, sing or chant a version of the Magnificat from the Book of Common Prayer or Common Worship: you will find it in the service of Evening Prayer.)

EXPLORE

Read

The flipside of the Magnificat is a protest chant. If Mary hadn't sung it in the joyful knowledge that God was doing all of these things, it could have come out as a list of desperate demands: "Scatter the proud! Bring down the mighty! Fill the hungry! Send away the rich! Help us, remember us, speak to us!" This song of praise has a heart of justice.

A friend and fellow writer, Clare Howard Weiner, painted an unusual picture of the Annunciation which first sparked this comparison for me.

The painting is titled 'Mary, Mary' and in it, Mary appears twice. One Mary is leading a student protest when Gabriel, a bright figure next to her, encounters her with his message.

'Mary, Mary: the Annunciation to Mary by the Angel Gabriel': Clare M.H. Weiner, 2016, original painting for inclusion in an Advent exhibtion at St Mary's Church, Conwy. Used by permission of the artist.

Looking at the painting, I imagine that the moment of the incarnation, so often depicted in medieval art with a shaft of light or the words of the angel entering Mary's ears, is here inextricably mixed with the passionate chants of the protestors; so that what starts to grow inside Mary is the fire of God's justice, God's plan for fixing the world.

. . .

The vision of a world in which the poor are fed while the rich are sent empty away resonates with the later words of Jesus about the last being first and the first last (Matthew 20:16) and whoever wishes to become great needing to serve (Mark 10:43-45). Mother and son have the same idea of a world turned on its head.

All this is borne out in Mary's own experience so far: she sings that God has looked on her 'low estate' and done great things for her (verses 48-49). From her confidence in what has been done for her, she looks out to the rest of the world. Indeed, in Weiner's painting, the second Mary stands in a window looking out on the protest: her baby son already hugged to her chest, she contemplates both her role and his in challenging the injustices of the world.

Like Mary, we can long for justice at the same time as being secure in the knowledge that God longs for, and works towards, the same goal; we can fight for change at the same time as recognising that justice will not be completely done until Jesus comes again. We praise God for what he has done, and is doing, in a turbulent world. That's the music of the Magnificat.

Discuss

- How can our confidence in God's mercy and justice stem from what he has done for us?
- What problem do you wish God would step in and solve straight away?
- Where do we get our ideas of what is just and unjust?
- Have you ever seen God's upside-down kingdom at work in the world? What does it look like?

Respond

For this response, you will need to spread out recent newspaper articles, pictures, headlines and clippings over a table or on the floor: perhaps every member of the group could bring some that had particularly caught their notice over the week. Try to have a mix of postive and negative news, as well as any protests and requests, examples of injustice and examples of people helping. Also have tealights and a means of lighting them (or use electric ones, which are safer). The lighting in the room needs to be good enough for everyone to see and read the newspapers.

Play some quiet music (A Touching Place by John Bell would work well for this) and encourage everyone to sit or move around contemplatively and take time to read the clippings. Imagine that Jesus is with you as you read, and think how he is reacting to each piece of news. When something particularly stirs up a reaction of compassion or anger for you, light a tealight and place it by those words or images as a continuing prayer.

When the music finishes, and everyone has returned to their place, say the Magnificat together.

UNTIL NEXT TIME

Pray

My soul is shouting that the Lord is great,
and all my heart is in this praise expressed:
for he has seen me in my low estate.
From now on, everyone will call me blessed.
For mighty God has done great things for me,
his mercy is for those who love his name,
for he has shown his strength and majesty,
the proud in heart have all been brought to shame.
The mighty have been toppled from their thrones,
the weak and feeble seated there instead:
the rich sent off with nothing, all alone,
the poor and hungry welcomed in and fed.
For God remembers what he said before:
His promise to his children, evermore.
Amen

Ponder

What does a Christian response to social injustice look like?

Prepare

For the next session, read Luke 2:8-15.

SESSION THREE:
GLORIA, A SONG OF PEACE

BEGIN

Introduction

The Gloria In Excelsis which we sing or say at communion services (although not during Advent, or Lent!) is an ancient Christian hymn, composed in maybe the third or fourth century as a 'private psalm': an early Christian poem written in the style of Biblical psalms. Its inspiration, as well as its first line, is clearly the song of the angels to the shepherds in Luke, and sometimes it goes by that title – 'Song of the Angels' – even though the rest of the song doesn't appear in the Bible passage. I can imagine the unknown writer meditating on the passage from Luke and wishing to extend the one line we are given for the angels' song into a full chorus of praise.

The message of the angels' song, however, is not only praise. In the original Greek, the short song seems to have a three-part structure. To God, glory; to earth, peace; among people, a word often translated 'goodwill' or 'favour' but also carrying the meaning of joy or delight. The angels' message is one of peace and reconciliation between heaven and earth. In this session, we will look into why that is, and what significance the song of the angels holds for us today.

OPENING QUESTION/ACTIVITY

What image, memory or activity do you associate with peace?

WORSHIP

Pray

Father, the angels sang to mark the moment when heaven reached out to earth. Help us to reach back to you now as we read, learn and talk together. Amen.

Sing

If you are feeling close enough to Christmas for carolling, there are plenty of carols that include the angels. It Came Upon A Midnight Clear goes particularly well with the content of this session, but you could also try While Shepherds Watched, Hark The Herald Angels Sing, Angels From The Realms of Glory or Nowell, Nowell (and your own favourites). Apart from carols, you could sing:

- To God be the Glory (Fanny Crosby)
- Holy, Holy, Holy, Lord God Almighty (Reginald Heber)
- O Worship the King (Robert Grant)
- Meekness and Majesty (Graham Kendrick)
- Peace, Perfect Peace Is The Gift (Kevin Mayhew)

Read

- Luke 2:8-15

JOIN THE SONG

For this section, the group will create a poem inspired by the song of the angels together. You will need three small slips of paper for each person – perhaps in three different colours for ease of reading them at the right moment – and everyone will need something to write with. The leader can also contribute lines as well as being the one to direct the poem at the end.

Ask everyone to think of three images or examples to write on their slips of paper. The first one should be an image of glory, the second an image of peace and the third an image of goodwill and kindness.

These can be single metaphors such as 'a sunset' or more developed examples, descriptions and memories such as 'the time I went star-gazing in the mountains' or 'when someone pays for someone else's shopping'. The only rule is to keep them short enough to be a single line of poetry (the size of the slips of paper helps with this!)

Once everyone has written their three lines, there are two ways to perform the poem. Either the leader gathers in everyone's writing and arranges it in sections beneath each stanza's opening line (see below) before reading it all out loud; or the leader reads the opening lines and invites everyone in turn to read their contribution for each section, then closes each section with the relevant word (see below) and opens the next one with the next opening line. The opening lines and an example of what the finished poem might sound like are given below.

Notes

The trick to leading this activity is helping everyone to understand what you're asking for without being too prescriptive. As a prompt, you could ask them 'Think of the last time you felt really peaceful,' or 'describe a peaceful scene,' or 'what does glory look like?' If people are struggling with the concept, you could show them the example below, but it's better to avoid giving lots of examples because that could either influence or take away from what the participants might have said. The best results happen when everyone writes more or less the first thing that comes to mind!

As with every activity that involves individuals writing things down, make especially sure that everyone knows their examples will be read out loud.

If your group is larger than about ten people, the poem will become long and unwieldy. In that case, you could split the group into three smaller groups and ask everyone for only one line each, so that group 1 then performs stanza 1, group 2 the next stanza and so on.

Opening lines

1. Glory to God in the highest, glory in every great thing! (At the end of the stanza, say: Glory!)
2. Peace on earth, may the whole earth know this peace: (At the end of the stanza, say: Peace!)
3. Among all people goodwill, kindness, grace: (At the end of the stanza, say: Grace!)

Example finished poem (I have imagined a small group of five people. Of course your poem may be much longer, or shorter!)

Glory to God in the highest, glory in every great thing!
The vastness of the universe
last night's sunset over the fields
when I found out how many times earth would fit inside the sun
a sudden strong gust of wind
thunderstorms
Glory!

Peace on earth, may the whole earth know this peace:
running water
my sleeping baby
an empty country church
the phonecall when I said sorry
feeling forgiven
Peace.

Among all people, goodwill, kindness, grace:
the woman who gave me her parking space
a smile from a friend
the food bank
the way my gran was always pleased to see me
a dog's wagging tail
Grace!

. . .

(Alternatively, you may like to say or sing the Gloria; although in Anglican and Catholic churches, the Gloria is not used during Lent or Advent.)

EXPLORE

Read

The ceasefire of Christmas 1914 has become an iconic moment in history, especially since its centenary in 2014 and that of the armistice in 2018. Peace descends between the trenches as two warring sides venture out to play football, exchange cigarettes and sing Silent Night, all surrounded by the misty magic of Christmas. It's even been made into a tear-jerking seasonal advertisement for a supermarket.

Is that what the angels meant when they sang about peace on earth? In the carol *It Came Upon The Midnight Clear*, written by Edmund Sears in 1849, the angels sing over a world of 'Babel sounds' and 'man, at war with man, hears not'. In the final stanza, Sears looks forward to a golden age of peace, as foretold in Isaiah 2 verse 4: 'Nation shall not life up sword against nation, neither shall they learn war any more'. This promise of a peaceful earth is certainly one way to interpret the message of the angels on Christmas night.

There is another way, too. The angels are God's ambassadors: their message of peace, instead of referring to peace between nations, is offering peace between humankind and God, an armistice between heaven and earth. Not that God has been warring against us, but that we have been rebelling – fighting – against God. Even though we are the instigators, the ones at odds, it is God in his generosity who steps into our territory by sending his son to offer a way back into a peaceful relationship. The image of the Christmas ceasefire does resonate with the song of the angels, but only if we imagine heaven in one trench and earth in the other.

This image is reflected throughout the Bible, from God's hanging up his bow in the heavens after Noah's flood (the word for 'bow' as in 'rainbow' is, in both Hebrew and English, also the kind of bow that shoots an arrow, and hanging it up indicates the end of war) to the parable Jesus tells about the owner of a vineyard sending his own son to the corrupt and violent tenants occupying it (Matthew 21:33-46).

I wonder if this meaning was in the mind of the early writer of the rest of the Gloria, who went on from the song of the angels to praise Jesus Christ 'who takes away the sins of the world – have mercy on us'?

Discuss

- What do you think the angels mean by 'peace to the earth'?
- Is the fact that the shepherds are the ones to receive the angels' message significant?
- How did the shepherds respond to the message?
- How can we respond to the same message today?

Respond

You will need: a Christmas card for each member of the group, with the song of the angels (Luke 2:14) written or pasted inside; extra blank cards, or paper, and pens.

The song of the angels is a simple and direct message from heaven to earth; from God to every one of us, like a Christmas card. With music playing, give everyone time to receive their card – perhaps by choosing it from the picture, perhaps just by passing them round – and to read the message slowly, several times, and take it in. Encourage everyone to imagine the message specifically addressed to them from God; perhaps they could write in their own names, and make a note of anything else that they feel God is saying to them as they read the message.

Then, using the blank cards or paper, give everyone time to reply to their card, as if they could hand a message back to the angels to deliver to God. They can do this in whatever way they wish; a few words of thanks, a question, a long letter or a picture; nobody else will see.

When people are ready, finish the session with a brief prayer asking God to see and accept the responses as prayer.

UNTIL NEXT TIME

Pray

Lord, you took a step into our world to make peace between heaven and earth. Forgive us for the times we've rejected you, turned away from you and ignored you. Help us to step back towards you. Thank you for your offer of peace and goodwill. Amen.

Ponder

How do we accept God's offer of peace?

Prepare

For next week, read Luke 2:22-38.

SESSION FOUR:
NUNC DIMITTIS, A SONG OF HOPE

BEGIN

Introduction

The story of Simeon singing the Nunc Dimittis comes right at the end of the Christmas and Epiphany seasons, at Candlemas. It's the last tale we hear about the infant Jesus. It's poignant because Simeon has received a personal promise from God that he will not die before seeing the Messiah; so he has been waiting in the temple for the fulfillment of a promise made to all humankind, but also very specifically to him. The opening words of his song acknowledge that he will now go peacefully to his death, knowing that the promise has been fulfilled; and it's remarkable that he is satisfied with the arrival of this forty-day old infant. He does not need to see Jesus performing miracles, nor does he need to hear him speak; it is enough for Simeon that the Messiah is here, on earth, with us.

Simeon's prophecy echoes Zechariah's song insofar as it recalls God's promises to Israel and uses the same metaphor of light. But it goes further, because Simeon mentions revelation to the Gentiles: he recognises Jesus as a saviour of all peoples, as the angels hinted in their song. So this final prophetic Christmas voice brings the others together in their declaration of who this child is and what he has come to do.

OPENING QUESTION/ACTIVITY

Imagine that you receive an angelic message: Jesus will meet you this afternoon in a local café. You decide to go and see: you go in, sit down, look around. How will you recognise Jesus?

WORSHIP

Pray

Lord Jesus, although you were a baby, Simeon recognised you; he welcomed you as a promise fulfilled, bringing peace for his life and death, and hope for the whole world. As we study his song, may we have faith in your presence with us; may we recognise your Spirit among us. Amen.

Sing

Here are some suggestions for hymns and songs which you could sing or listen to as you worship together:

- Christ, be our light! (Bernadette Farrell)
- The Candle Song (Like a candle flame) (Graham Kendrick)
- Thou whose almighty word (John Marriott)

Read

- Luke 2:22-38

JOIN THE SONG

This spoken piece layers the three other songs over Simeon's song by noticing echoes from each and aligning them together. It is most effective spoken out loud as a group: give individuals or pairs (or a small group in the case of the angels) a part each, depending on your numbers. If you can, make Simeon's part distinctive (perhaps by being the only single voice speaking, or the only group, or just the loudest!)

All the individual lines here are taken from the NRSV, but obviously they do not appear in order, and I haven't always been able to preserve the punctuation exactly, for the purposes of arranging them as a poem in this way.

Simeon: Simeon took Jesus in his arms and praised God.
Zechariah: Blessed be the Lord God of Israel,
Mary: My soul magnifies the Lord, and my spirit rejoices in God my Saviour,
Angels: Glory to God in the highest heaven!
Simeon: Master, now you are dismissing your servant in peace,
Angels: peace among those whom he favours
Simeon: according to your word;
Mary: according to the promise he made to our ancestors,

Zechariah: the oath that he swore to our ancestor Abraham,
Mary: to Abraham and to his descendants forever.
Simeon: For my eyes have seen your salvation,
Mary: for the Mighty One has done great things for me,
Zechariah: He has raised up a mighty saviour for us
Mary: he has looked with favour on the lowliness of his servant
Angels: on earth peace among those whom he favours.
Simeon: your salvation, which you have prepared in the presence of all peoples,
Angels: good news of great joy for all the people
Mary: from now on all generations will call me blessed;
Simeon: a light for revelation to the Gentiles
Zechariah: to give light to those who sit in darkness and in the shadow of death
Simeon: and for glory to your people Israel.
Mary: He has helped his servant Israel
Zechariah: in the house of his servant David
Angels: To you is born this day in the city of David a saviour
Zechariah: a mighty saviour
Mary: God my Saviour
Simeon: my eyes have seen your salvation.

(Alternatively, you may like to use this space to say, sing or chant a version of the Nunc Dimittis from the Book of Common Prayer or Common Worship: you will find it in the service of Evening Prayer.)

EXPLORE

Read

The main thing we know about Simeon from Luke's description of him is that he was a man unusually in tune with God. Luke writes that Simeon was 'righteous and devout, waiting for the consolation of Israel, and the Holy Spirit was upon him' (verse 25). The Spirit's communication to Simeon is not only in the understanding that he will not die before seeing the Christ, but Luke says that the Spirit led Simeon into the temple that day (verse 27) and so we understand that from the moment he sees Jesus, every word from Simeon's mouth is Spirit-filled. This fulfillment of what may have been long years of waiting pours out as a song at first, but Simeon's prophetic insights continue beyond his song in what he says to Mary, which shows something of an understanding of what must happen to Jesus.

Simeon is unusual, because he sees the end from the very beginning. Zechariah, Mary and the angels have recalled God's promises in their songs, and they have declared their fulfillment: their songs are full of joy and excitement for a new world, without knowing exactly how that world will come about. But Simeon's song strikes a quieter, more unsettling note. It's the song of a man who knows he is about to die; when he holds the infant Jesus, he knows that he is holding life and death together. There will be falling as well as rising, he says; and a sword will pierce Mary's heart, too.

Simeon's song is one of hope, but hope is bittersweet, because we can only ever hope for things that we can't yet reach. Yet as Simeon unfailingly knows, to hope in the certainty of God's promises is enough. Both his song and his prophecy begin with death, but look forward to peace, salvation, light and glory.

. . .

Discuss

- When we consider the darkness of the world, what sparks hope?
- Is it ever possible to be 100% certain in matters of faith?
- Is there anything you know for sure?
- People often say jokingly, "Ah, I can die happy now." What would 'dying happy' look like for you?

Respond

Gather everyone around a traditional crib scene so that they can all see. Darken the room and light a single candle within or in front of the crib. Give each individual an unlit candle.

If the group feels comfortable doing so together, encourage them to share prayer requests openly. If they prefer, share some quiet time in the darkness, asking them to name their requests silently.

You could listen to the carol *Mary, Did You Know*, (by Mark Lowry; Pentatonix has an excellent version) or to Graham Kendrick's *Thorns In The Straw*, or to any sung version of the Nunc Dimittis.

Finally, light a candle from the single one burning, and pass the light around until everyone's candles are lit, saying to one another "The light and hope of Christ" as you share the flame.

UNTIL NEXT TIME

Pray

Christ our Lord, you are light in darkness; help us to shine as lights in the darkness of the world. You are our consolation in times of pain and trouble; help us to console others. Give us your peace to face life and death, as you did for Simeon; may we look forward with him to the hope of everlasting life in you. Amen.

Ponder

Which of the four songs most reflects the way you feel when you think about Jesus at Christmas?

WORKSHOP SESSION

Preparation

Mince pies, mulled wine and Christmas music in the background are all appropriate for this fun and creative session!

See the workshop activities below for suggestions of how to set out separate areas for the writing of each song.

A whiteboard, flipchart or some large sheets of paper and thick pens will help with collecting ideas for the opening activity, and later if you're working as a group.

For the final celebration, you will need carol books and backing tracks or recordings to sing along to.

Table 1:

Nouns	Verbs	Adjectives
soul	magnifies	humble
spirit	rejoices	blessed
strength	exalted	mighty
remembrance	filled	holy
mercy	helped	hungry
generations	promised	rich
people	visited	proud
salvation	redeemed	tender
servant	saved	favoured
prophets	swore	good
covenant	delivered	great
holiness	remember	highest
righteousness	guide	
fear	prepared	
knowledge		
forgiveness		
sunrise		
light		
peace		
revelation		
glory		

Table 2: Names of Jesus

Saviour
Light of the World
Bread of Heaven
Good Shepherd
Lion of Judah
Lamb
Lord (Adonai)
Son of David
Word
Prince of Peace
Root/Shoot of Jesse
Messiah (Christ)

OPENING DISCUSSION AND ACTIVITY

What are your favourite Christmas carols? Do you love them for the tune, the lyrics, the associated memories?

Choose one, and make a quick list of the main words and imagery used. For example, if I chose *Away In A Manger*, I might write: manger, crib, bed, little, sweet, stars, hay, quiet...

Compare notes with the rest of the group. What words and images stand out in our popular carols?

Compare the lists with the words in Table 1 above. What are the differences in focus and imagery between the songs in Luke and our favourite carols?

WORKSHOP ACTIVITIES - WRITE A SONG

The options given below, which are prompts rather than strict instructions, could be set out in separate areas for people to move around individually and have a go at several; or they could be presented for the group to choose one; or the leader could decide to choose just one or two for the group to work on together. This will depend on the size and confidence of the group.

Before you begin, make sure that everyone understands that these 'songs' do not have to look like songs! They are prompts for spontaneous shouts of praise just like the ones in Luke's Gospel. They don't have to rhyme or scan or have verses, let alone tunes, unless their writer particularly wants them to. The following are all just suggestions of ways to structure words and ideas both prayerfully and playfully. If they spark something completely different, that's fine too.

Write a song of salvation

(If you are setting out individual areas for this session, set out these instructions alongside a copy of the Benedictus.)

Zechariah's song remembers God's saving goodness in the past, and looks forward to a promise of salvation in the future.

Think of three times in the past that you have felt saved or rescued, or experienced God's goodness, and write them down. These could include your journey into faith, your baptism, or people who have helped you; they could be spiritual or practical.

Zechariah begins with 'Blessed be the Lord...for he has...redeemed his people' so you could begin with a similar statement of praise.

Then write your three ideas, beginning each time with 'He has...' or 'God has...'

Then write two or three hopes for the future, beginning each with 'He will...' or 'He has promised that...' These could be things personal to you, or as in Zechariah's song, a vision of what God wants to do with the future of his people.

Write a song of justice

(If you are setting out individual areas for this session, set these instructions alongside the newspaper clippings and images from session 2 and a copy of the Magnificat.)

The arrival of God on earth as a tiny baby was the beginning of everything Mary sang about, the world order turned upside down: the powerful made weak and the humble lifted up.

The Magnificat has a structure of opposites: up and down, proud and humble, rich and poor, full and empty. Make your own list of opposites based on examples of where justice is needed today. Some of them might be the same, and others more specific. For example: comfortable and homeless, powerful and exploited, slave and owner, addicted and dealer.

Begin your song, like Mary, with 'My soul magnifies the Lord, because...'

Then, using your list, imagine that God has already overturned these examples of injustice, and like Mary, list them in the past tense, for example, 'He has rescued the slaves from their owner; he has housed the refugee and sent the comfortable out in the rain' and so on.

Finish with 'As he promised when...' and an example of how the Christmas story shows this overturning. For example: 'As he promised when he sent his son as a baby' or 'As he promised when the angels announced the good news to the shepherds' and so on.

. . .

Write a song of peace (and praise)

(If you are setting out individual areas for this session, set out these instructions alongside an image of angels or a Christmas crib scene, a copy of the Gloria and some copies of the song of the angels (Luke 2:14) in several different translations/versions: try Biblehub.com to help with this. If you choose to use the 'Join The Song' activity from session 3, then also put out paper with the three headings and verse endings, leaving space for the lines to be written in between.)

Your song of peace could use the group exercise given under 'Join the Song' in session three. This would work especially well if you didn't do it as part of that session, or if you used it as a group but could now have a go at the same method individually.

Alternatively, work in the way of the ancient writer of the first Gloria, and take the brief song of the angels as the first line of your own meditation or prayer, thanking and praising God for sending Jesus, and writing about how the promise of peace and reconciliation between heaven and earth has changed the world – or, more personally, how it has changed or is changing your life.

Write a song of hope

(If you are setting out individual areas for this session, set out these instructions alongside an image of Simeon, a copy of the Nunc Dimittis and some candles or electric candles.)

Simeon's song and prophecy moves from death and darkness towards light and life, but still acknowledges the pain to come.

Try writing this one from the perspective of a person who is in a dark place: someone who is grieving, or unwell or depressed. Perhaps that person is you, or perhaps you can imagine them. Begin the song, or each line of the song, from that place. For example, you might use the structure 'Because Jesus was born, I can hope that...' or 'Now that I believe God is with us, I can imagine that one day...' Write a few lines that way, reaching from a place of darkness towards a vision of hope, however distant.

Simeon grounds his hope in what he sees in front of him: 'for my eyes *have seen* your salvation'. See if you can finish your song with a more definite statement of 'I know' 'I believe' or 'I have seen'.

Write a song of your own

(If you are setting out individual areas for this session, set out these instructions alongside some Bibles, copies of tables 1 and 2 above and copies of all four songs, as well as an assortment of nativity images – Christmas cards would be an easy way to do that.)

. . .

It may be that you would rather write your own thoughts on what Christmas and the nativity story means to you. If so, go for it!

It can help to gather thoughts and words before beginning. You could fill out your own table, like Table 1 above, of words arranged into nouns, verbs and adjectives, or simply make a list of images that come to mind. You could also use the list given in Table 2 of names and images for Jesus, thinking about which ones chime or contrast with the image of Jesus as an infant.

You could also read the four songs, or the Christmas story in Luke 2, and gather some favourite words or phrases from them, in the same way that Zechariah, Mary and Simeon's songs all echo words and ideas from earlier scriptures.

Once you have made some notes of the words and images that most appeal to you, you could choose an image of the nativity and describe what you see, weaving those words into your description.

Celebration

Once the workshop time is over, come back together for a final time of worship. Alternate singing Christmas carols together with hearing the songs of anybody who wishes to share what they wrote in the session.

Final prayer

Lord, we thank you for what we have learned and discovered this Advent through reading the words of praise that were sung when you first came to earth. We thank you for the singers of those ancient songs, and that through you, Lord Jesus, we can join our own songs with them and reach the ears of our Father in heaven. May you accept all our words and thoughts of praise, peace and hope; and be with us all this Christmas and evermore. Amen.